Healthy Fast Foods

Mason Crest
450 Parkway Drive, Suite D
Broomall, PA 19008
www.masoncrest.com

Printed and bound in the United States of America.

First printing
9 8 7 6 5 4 3 2 1

Series ISBN: 978-1-4222-2874-6
Hardcover ISBN: 978-1-4222-2879-1
ebook ISBN: 978-1-4222-8941-9
Paperback ISBN: 978-1-4222-2988-0

The Library of Congress has cataloged the
      hardcopy format(s) as follows:

Library of Congress Cataloging-in-Publication Data

Etingoff, Kim.
  Healthy fast foods / Kim Etingoff.
    pages cm. – (Understanding nutrition : a gateway to physical & mental health)
  Audience: Grade 4 to 6.
  ISBN 978-1-4222-2879-1 (hardcover) – ISBN 978-1-4222-2874-6 (series) – ISBN 978-1-4222-
2988-0 (paperback) – ISBN 978-1-4222-8941-9 (ebook)
  1. Convenience foods–Juvenile literature. 2. Fast food restaurants–Juvenile literature. 3. Children–Nutrition–Juvenile literature. 4. Nutrition–Juvenile literature. 5. Health–Juvenile literature. I. Title.
  TX370.E85 2014
  642'.1–dc23
                                2013009802

Produced by Vestal Creative Services.
www.vestalcreative.com

UNDERSTANDING NUTRITION:
A GATEWAY TO PHYSICAL AND MENTAL HEALTH

Healthy Fast Foods

KIM ETINGOFF

Mason Crest

CONTENTS

INTRODUCTION
by Dr. Joshua Borus

There are many decisions to make about food. Almost everyone wants to "eat healthy"—but what does that really mean? What is the "right" amount of food and what is a "normal" portion size? Do I need sports drinks if I'm an athlete—or is water okay? Are all "organic" foods healthy? Getting reliable information about nutrition can be confusing. All sorts of restaurants and food makers spend billions of dollars trying to get you to buy their products, often by implying that a food is "good for you" or "healthy." Food packaging has unbiased, standardized nutrition labels, but if you don't know what to look for, they can be hard to understand. Magazine articles and the Internet seem to always have information about the latest fad diets or new "superfoods" but little information you can trust. Finally, everyone's parents, friends, and family have their own views on what is healthy. How are you supposed to make good decisions with all this information when you don't know how to interpret it?

The goal of this series is to arm you with information to help separate what is healthy from not healthy. The books in the series will help you think about things like proper portion size and how eating well can help you stay healthy, improve your mood, and manage your weight. These books will also help you take action. They will let you know some of the changes you can make to keep healthy and how to compare eating options.

Keep in mind a few broad rules:

- First, healthy eating is a lifelong process. Learning to try new foods, preparing foods in healthy ways, and focusing on the big picture are essential parts of that process. Almost no one can keep on a very restrictive diet for a long time or entirely cut out certain groups of foods, so it's best to figure out how to eat healthy in a way that's realistic for you by making a number of small changes.

- Second, a lot of healthy eating hasn't really changed much over the years and isn't that complicated once you know what to look for. The core of a healthy diet is still eating reasonable portions at regular meals. This should be mostly fruits and vegetables, reasonable amounts of proteins, and lots of whole grains, with few fried foods or extra fats. "Junk food" and sweets also have their place—they taste good and have a role in celebrations and other happy events—but they aren't meant to be a cornerstone of your diet!

- Third, avoid drinks with calories in them, beverages like sodas, iced tea, and most juices. Try to make your liquid intake all water and you'll be better off.

- Fourth, eating shouldn't be done mindlessly. Often people will munch while they watch TV or play games because it's something to do or because they're bored rather then because they are hungry. This can lead to lots of extra food intake, which usually isn't healthy. If you are eating, pay attention, so that you are enjoying what you eat and aware of your intake.

- Finally, eating is just one part of the equation. Exercise every day is the other part. Ideally, do an activity that makes you sweat and gets your heart beating fast for an hour a day—but even making small decisions like taking stairs instead of elevators or walking home from school instead of driving make a difference.

After you read this book, don't stop. Find out more about healthy eating. Choosemyplate.gov is a great Internet resource from the U.S. government that can be trusted to give good information; www.hsph.harvard.edu/nutritionsource is a webpage from the Harvard School of Public Health where scientists sort through all the data about food and nutrition and distill it into easy-to-understand messages. Your doctor or nurse can also help you learn more about making good decisions. You might also want to meet with a nutritionist to get more information about healthy living.

Food plays an important role in social events, informs our cultural heritage and traditions, and is an important part of our daily lives. It's not just how we fuel our bodies; it's also but how we nourish our spirit. Learn how to make good eating decisions and build healthy eating habits—and you'll have increased long-term health, both physically and psychologically.

So get started now!

1

Fast-Food Obsession

Fast food is everywhere. You drive or walk by fast-food restaurants a few times a day. You see fast-food ads on TV and on billboards. Maybe you eat in a fast-food restaurant once a week—or more.

All that fast food adds up though, negatively affecting our health. In fact, fast food is some of the worst food you can eat when it comes to health.

Yet people keep eating fast food because it's so easy to get—it's fast, after all!—and it tastes so good. Sometimes, it seems like the world is **obsessed** with fast food.

Fast-food restaurants make getting food as easy as can be. You don't even have to leave your car to order your burger and fries. For many people, getting food quickly is more important than eating healthy food, but there are consequences from eating too much fast food.

Defining Fast Food

Fast food is any food that is made very quickly in a restaurant. People eat all sorts of fast foods, like hamburgers, tacos, sandwiches, french fries, and soda. In general, fast foods are not healthy foods.

In fast-food restaurants, waiters don't come over to your table to take your order. You walk up to a counter and tell the cashier what you want. You usually order off a menu posted behind the counter.

Fast-food restaurants are usually chains. Chain restaurants have locations in lots of different places. One restaurant in a chain looks almost exactly like another. However, some fast-food restaurants aren't part of a chain.

People who order fast food eat it quickly, or they take it with them to eat somewhere else. Many fast-food places have a drive-through, where drivers can pull up to a window and order food. Then they take it away with them to eat at home or on the road.

So What's with Fast Food?

Fast food is popular. Fast-food restaurants serve millions of meals and snacks every day, all around the world. Just about everyone in the world has gone to a fast-food restaurant at one point or another.

Why do people go to fast-food restaurants so often? What makes them so popular? First, they're very convenient. They're called "fast food" because you get your food quickly! For busy people on the go, fast food may seem like the only way to eat. They can pull up to the drive-through, order, and get their food, all in less than five minutes. Fast food seems like a great idea for families on the run, or people who don't have time to sit down and eat a meal.

> ## What Does It Mean If You're Obsessed?
>
> When people say that someone is **obsessed** with something, they usually mean that person thinks about the thing all the time. Whatever it is, it's constantly on the person's mind.

Eating fast food every once in a while is fine, but if you find yourself choosing fast food over healthier food all the time, you should think about cutting back. Eating too much fast food can lead to health problems and weight gain.

Fast food also appeals to people who don't know how to cook very well. Some people never learn how to cook properly or just don't enjoy cooking. Instead of making a meal at home, they eat out. Fast-food restaurants take the stress out of food preparation.

Fast-food restaurants are also familiar. If you travel to a new place, you know the fast-food places will be exactly the same as at home. Eating at a Subway® in Maine will be exactly the same as eating at a Subway in California. McDonald's® food is the same in Florida as it is in Oregon. A lot of people like to stick with food they know—and that often means fast food. You know what you're getting when you order.

Fast food also seems cheap. When people eat out, they often don't want to spend tons of money. Parents with kids can't always afford to pay for restaurant meals for their family—but fast food offers meals under $5. Compared to sit-down restaurant meals that can cost $20 or more, fast food is a much cheaper choice.

Fast Food By the Numbers

We eat out a lot! About half of all the money people spend on food is spent at restaurants. The other half is spent at grocery stores or farmers' markets, buying food to fix at home. A lot of money spent at restaurants is spent at fast-food restaurants. On any given day, one out of every three people in America will eat at a fast-food restaurant. In Australia, each person eats the equivalent of one Burger King Whopper® every day. A study done in 2005 on 15 nations around the world, found that in 12 out of the 15 countries, most people preferred to eat fast food instead of other restaurant meals or homemade meals.

POTATOES

The potato can be a high calorie food or a low calorie food, based on how it is prepared.

500 cal
A large order of McDonald's french fries

300 cal
A packet of potato crisps

111 cal
half-cup of mashed potatoes with milk and butter

220 cal
white baked potato, with skin

117 cal
sweet baked potato with skin

145 cal
white baked potato, without skin

144 cal
Newmedium piece of candied sweet potato

Potatoes are usually very healthy, but when they're made into french fries or potato chips, the number of calories in those foods is much higher than in a baked potato.

Many people also think fast food tastes good. They go because they like eating the food. Fast food is really high in salt, fat, and sugar. These are all things people crave. Our bodies are made to think they taste good. Unfortunately, salt, fat, and sugar aren't actually healthy when people eat them in large amounts. Hamburgers and fries have a lot of fat and salt. Soda and ice cream have lots of sugar. Our bodies crave all that fat, salt, and sugar—but too much is unhealthy!

Fast Food Ads

Another reason people eat so much fast food is because they see ads for it all the time. Think about all the TV, magazine, and online ads you see. If you kept track for a day, how many ads for fast-food restaurants do you think you would see?

Scientists have figured out elementary-school aged kids see about four TV fast food ads every day. Older kids and teens see five fast food ads every day. Every day you watch TV, you'll probably see ads for any of the big fast-food chains.

And TV ads aren't the only place you see advertisements. The sides of buses have ads. Billboards have ads. Websites like Facebook have ads. Everywhere you turn, someone is trying to sell you something—and sometimes they're trying to sell you fast food.

Fast-food places spend lots of money on ads. They know people will remember the restaurant if they see ads for it over and over again. When you see an ad for Burger King, does it make you want to go? Maybe you suddenly get a craving for french fries. Even if you don't, you file the ad away in your brain. The ad reminds you Burger King exists. In a couple days, you may remember and want to go to Burger King.

Fast food is everywhere, all around the world, and lots of people are eating it. However, eating at a fast-food restaurant isn't the healthiest decision. Before you decide to take a trip to your favorite fast-food restaurant, take some time to learn the facts.

2

The Problem with Fast Food

The problem with fast food is that it's unhealthy. You've probably heard that before, and may have ignored the warning. After all, if everyone is eating at fast-food restaurants, how bad can the food be? If you don't know what makes fast food unhealthy, you won't know to how to make smart decisions about eating it.

Dietary Fat

Unsaturated Fat

Food Examples

Almonds
Vegetables
Fish
Olives
Olive Oil

Benefits

Works in conjunction
with saturated fats
to prevent heart attacks
and strokes

Raises good
cholesterol levels

Saturated Fat

Food Examples

Beef
Butter
Pizza
Ice Cream
Lard

Benefits

Works in conjunction
with unsaturated fats
to prevent heart attacks
and strokes

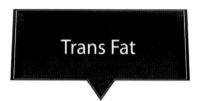

Trans Fat

Food Examples

Cookies
Donuts
Cakes
Fries
Hydrogenated Oil

Benefits

None

There are three kinds of fat in the foods we eat. While we need some fat in our diet, trans fat is very unhealthy and should be avoided whenever possible.

Salt, Sugar, and More

Fast foods are unhealthy partly because they have three very unhealthy things in them: salt, sugar, and unhealthy fat.

Lots of fast foods are particularly high in salt. French fries are dusted with it. Hamburger and cheeseburgers have salt mixed in. Dips and dressings have a lot of salt. It's hard to stay away from salt in a fast-food restaurant!

People actually do need to eat a little salt every day. Salt helps keep the balance of water in our bodies just right. Too much salt, though, is dangerous. Most people end up eating too much salt every day, and fast food doesn't help.

Eating too much salt makes people feel **bloated**. This is a sign that the water in their bodies is out of balance. People who eat too much salt might also feel thirsty all the time.

A bigger problem, though, is the long-term costs of eating a lot of salt. Too much salt in the diet leads to heart disease, including heart attacks. It also increases a person's chance of having a **stroke**. Even kids can have **high blood pressure** if they eat too much salt. And later on, high blood pressure can lead to heart disease.

Sugar is another unhealthy ingredient in fast foods. You can find sugar in lots of fast foods and drinks—soda, ice cream, rolls, and even ketchup.

What Does Feeling Bloated Mean?

When people say they feel **bloated**, they meant that their bodies feel puffy and swollen. They feel like they're suddenly fatter than they really are. Their clothes may fit more tightly than usual, or the rings on their fingers may be tighter.

What Is a Stroke?

When people say that someone had a **stroke**, they mean that the blood flow inside the person's brain was interrupted for some reason. When this happens, brain cells die. Afterward, the person may not be able to speak or move normally. If too many brain cells are killed, the person will die.

What Is High Blood Pressure?

You need blood pressure to live. Without it, your blood wouldn't be able to move through your body. Your blood carries oxygen and food to all your body's cells. Your blood pushing against your blood vessel walls as your heart pumps causes blood pressure. Blood pressure rises with each heartbeat and falls when the heart relaxes between beats, but there is always a certain amount of pressure in the arteries. Activity and rest, as well as temperature, diet, emotional state, posture, and medications affect blood pressure. When a person has **high blood pressure**, their blood pushes too hard against their blood vessel walls. This means that the heart must pump harder and the arteries must carry blood that's moving under greater pressure. If high blood pressure continues for a long time, the heart and arteries may no longer work as well as they should. Other body organs, including the kidneys, eyes, and brain may also be affected.

People need sugar, just like they need salt. Sugar gives the body energy, which it uses to move, think, breathe, and live. But just like salt, too much sugar is unhealthy.

In the short run, too much sugar can give you headaches. It can mess with your digestion, and give you stomachaches or make you feel bloated.

In the long run, eating a lot of sugar leads to weight gain. Scientists also think it is one thing that it can cause heart disease, skin problems, and **cancer**. That's a long list of diseases for a little sugar!

The third thing that makes fast foods unhealthy is fat. Fats are divided into healthy fats, called unsaturated fats, and unhealthy fats. The unhealthy kinds of fat are called saturated and trans fats.

Healthy fats are important. The body needs them to keep organs protected and absorb vitamins. Avocados, vegetable oil, and nuts have healthy unsaturated fats in them.

Unhealthy fats are not so great. Meat, dairy, margarine, and fried foods—foods that are common in fast foods—have saturated and trans fats. Burgers, onion rings, and nacho chips are all sources of unhealthy fats.

Saturated and trans fats are bad for the circulatory system, including the heart. They affect your blood **cholesterol** in an unhealthy way. Unhealthy blood cholesterol leads to heart and artery disease. However, some scientists claim saturated fats in particular might not be as bad as we think. For now, though, it's best to limit them.

Calories and Weight Gain

One of the very first things that happens when a person eats a lot of fast food (or too much food in general) is weight gain. Weight gain happens when a person eats too many calories.

Calories are the way we measure the energy in food. Without energy from food, we couldn't move around, breathe, or even think. Calories are how we measure that energy. A food with 500 calories has a lot of energy. A food with only 75 calories has much less.

What Is Cancer?

Cancer is a disease that causes cells in your body to divide and grow faster than normal. These abnormal cells can make tumors that may grow larger and larger. The tumors can keep healthy cells and body organs from doing their job.

What Is Cholesterol?

Cholesterol is a waxy substance. You need some to help your brain, skin, and other organs grow and do their jobs. But too much can float around in your blood and build up on the walls of your blood vessels. If a lot of cholesterol collects on the blood vessel walls, it's a little like when the pipes in your kitchen sink get clogged with food and other junk. If your blood vessels get clogged with cholesterol, it can cause a heart attack or stroke.

What Are Consequences?

Consequences are things that happen because you did something else. The consequence of being nicer to your brother or sister might be that you fight less. The consequence of drinking too much alcohol is getting drunk. The consequence of eating too much food is often weight gain.

Calories aren't bad. As long as people get around 2,000 calories a day, they shouldn't worry. Eating more than 2,000 calories a day (and not exercising to burn them up) is a problem though. That's when people gain weight. On the other hand, eating fewer than 2,000 calories a day usually makes people lose weight.

Fast food has a lot of calories. One fast-food meal can have more than 1,000 calories. For example, a Big Mac® from McDonald's has 550 calories. Add on a large order of fries and a soda, and you've eaten 1,300 calories total—more than half of what you need to eat in a whole day. And you only ate one meal!

All those calories cause weight gain. And weighing too much is unhealthy for a lot of reasons. Moving around becomes hard when you are overweight. Bones and joints have a hard time carrying a lot of weight, and they get damaged. Heart problems and strokes are more common. A lot can go wrong when someone is overweight.

People who are overweight are often embarrassed about it. They think they're ugly or stupid for weighing too much. That's not a good way of looking at it, though. People aren't bad if they're overweight—but they should think about losing weight if they want to live a long and healthy life!

Diabetes

One of the most serious **consequences** of eating fast food, or too much unhealthy food in general, is diabetes.

Diabetes is a disease that gets in the way of how your body gets energy from sugar. Sugar provides energy for the body. Think about how a gasoline makes a car run. Food—

including sugar—makes the human body run. The sugar from the food you eat eventually makes its way from your digestive system to your blood—and then it gets carried to all your body cells. Your cells use it for energy. The key to moving the sugar from the blood to the cells is called insulin. It's the chemical that helps glucose enter the body's cells, where it can be used for energy or stored for future use.

In a person with diabetes, their body doesn't have enough insulin. Or the person's cells ignore the insulin and it doesn't work right. This person has a kind of diabetes called type 2 diabetes.

Scientists aren't sure exactly what causes type 2 diabetes. They do know that people who are overweight get diabetes much more often than people with a healthy weight.

People with diabetes have to be careful about what they eat, and they have to make sure to exercise. They are also more at risk for heart disease, strokes, and other illnesses. Diabetes can lead to eye problems and kidney failure too. It's a serious disease.

Eating too much fast food is one thing that can lead to weight gain. And weight gain might lead to diabetes. So limiting how much fast food you eat is one way to avoid this diesease!

A Sometimes Food

You can safely eat fast food once in a while. One fast-food meal won't really do you any harm. A fast-food meal every other day, though, is really unhealthy.

Type 1 Diabetes

Most people with diabetes have type 2 diabetes. Both adults and kids can get type 2 diabetes. The other kind of diabetes is called type 1 diabetes. Type 1 happens when the body doesn't actually make enough insulin. People have to give themselves shots of insulin and choose what they eat very carefully. Usually kids and young adults are diagnosed with type 1 diabetes.

Description, Analysis is based on one Burger	Calories	Fat (g)
Burger King, Hamburger	333	15
Burger King, Cheeseburger	380	20
Burger King, Cheeseburger, Whopper Jr	460	27
Burger King, Hamburger, Whopper	678	37
Burger King, Cheeseburger, Whopper	790	48
Burger King, Cheeseburger, Double Whopper	1061	68
McDonald's Hamburger	265	10
McDonald's Cheeseburger	313	14
McDonald's Hamburger, Quarter Pounder	417	20
McDonald's Cheeseburger, Big Mac	563	33
McDonald's Cheeseburger, Quarter Pounder, double	734	45
Wendy's, Hamburger, jr	284	10
Wendy's, Hamburger, classic single	464	23
Wendy's, Cheeseburger, classic single	522	27
Wendy's, Hamburger, Big Bacon Classic	570	29
Wendy's, Cheeseburger, classic double	747	44
White Castle, Hamburger, Slyder	140	7
White Castle, Cheeseburger	160	9
White Castle, Cheeseburger, double	290	18
White Castle, Cheeseburger, bacon, double	360	23

Many fast-food restaurants serve foods that have a lot of calories in them. One burger can have up to 1,000 calories in it. That's about half of the number of calories a person is meant to eat each day!

So save fast foods for special occasions. If your friend is having a birthday party at a fast-food restaurant, go ahead and eat what you'd like. Just don't go back the next day and do the same thing.

No food is so unhealthy you can't ever eat it. Foods can be unhealthy when you eat them all the time. Then, over time, all the unhealthy stuff in food can add up and make you sick or make you gain weight. Keep fast foods as sometimes foods, and you'll be making a healthy choice.

The alternative to eating unhealthy is eating healthy, of course. Eating healthy doesn't have to be hard—or gross either!

3

Healthy Eating

S ure, fast food is unhealthy, but you might not think the alternative is very appetizing. For some people, healthy eating seems weird or yucky. They think of endless meals of tofu and boiled broccoli.

But eating healthy can be delicious, and just as easy as grabbing a fast-food meal. Healthy eating is a way to take care of your body, and it can make you look and feel good.

Eating Fruits and Veggies

You've heard it before—"Eat your fruits and veggies." You hear it because it's true! Eating fruits and vegetables is an important part of eating healthy.

Nutrition Facts

Serving Size   1 Cup (53g/1.9 oz.)
Servings Per Container   About 8

Amount Per Serving

Calories 190	Calories from Fat 25

	% Daily Value*
Total Fat 3g	**5%**
Saturated Fat 0g	**0%**
Trans Fat 0g	
Cholesterol 0mg	**0%**
Sodium 100mg	**4%**
Potassium 300mg	**9%**
Total Carbohydrate 37g	**12%**
Dietary Fiber 8g	**32%**
Soluble Fiber	
Insoluble Fiber	
Sugars 13g	
Protein 9g	**14%**

Vitamin A 0%	C 0%

You can find out how much sugar, salt, and fat is in the food you eat by reading food labels. Many fast-food restaurants have nutrition facts on their websites.

Fruits and vegetables have a lot of **nutrients** in them. People need nutrients to grow and stay healthy. The body can't make nutrients itself, so it has to get them from somewhere else. That somewhere else is food.

Nutrients do different things inside your body. Calcium, a mineral, keeps bones strong and healthy. Vitamin A works with the eyes and helps you see well. Protein keeps muscles strong.

What Are Nutrients?

Nutrients are the substances in food that your body needs to live and grow. Vitamins, minerals, protein, carbohydrates, and fats are all different kind of nutrients.

Fruits and vegetables happen to have a lot of nutrients. When you eat them, your body enjoys the positive effects of nutrients. One of the problems with fast food is that it doesn't have these nutrients. Or it has too many of the wrong ones, like unhealthy fats.

Eating fruits and vegetables doesn't have to be a chore. Eat fruit at breakfast and as a snack. Grabbing an apple or banana on the go is a good way to get in an extra serving of fruit. Stick vegetables into your sandwiches. Blend a smoothie with berries.

Try new fruits and vegetables you've never had before. You never know what you'll like. Sticking to fresh or frozen fruits is the healthiest choice. Canned fruits often have extra sugar, and canned vegetables usually have extra salt.

Try Whole Grains

Whole grains are healthier for you than non-whole grains. All grains are seeds from grass plants, including rice, oats, and wheat. Each grain seed has three parts to it. Non-whole grains only have one part left. Factories take out the other parts so the grains will last longer on the shelf. Also, sometimes people think that white bread and rice look better than brown.

Whole grains have all three parts. And all those parts have good nutrients in them, like fiber and protein. Non-whole grains don't have as many of those nutrients because they've been taken out.

A SIP OF SODA: HOW SOFT DRINKS IMPACT YOUR HEALTH

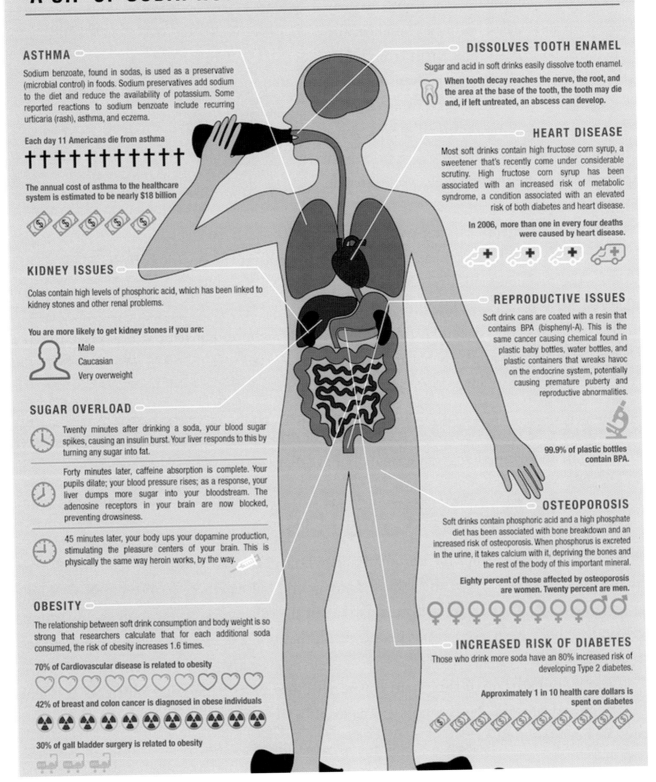

ASTHMA

Sodium benzoate, found in sodas, is used as a preservative (microbial control) in foods. Sodium preservatives add sodium to the diet and reduce the availability of potassium. Some reported reactions to sodium benzoate include recurring urticaria (rash), asthma, and eczema.

Each day 11 Americans die from asthma

✝✝✝✝✝✝✝✝✝✝✝

The annual cost of asthma to the healthcare system is estimated to be nearly $18 billion

KIDNEY ISSUES

Colas contain high levels of phosphoric acid, which has been linked to kidney stones and other renal problems.

You are more likely to get kidney stones if you are:

Male
Caucasian
Very overweight

SUGAR OVERLOAD

Twenty minutes after drinking a soda, your blood sugar spikes, causing an insulin burst. Your liver responds to this by turning any sugar into fat.

Forty minutes later, caffeine absorption is complete. Your pupils dilate; your blood pressure rises; as a response, your liver dumps more sugar into your bloodstream. The adenosine receptors in your brain are now blocked, preventing drowsiness.

45 minutes later, your body ups your dopamine production, stimulating the pleasure centers of your brain. This is physically the same way heroin works, by the way.

OBESITY

The relationship between soft drink consumption and body weight is so strong that researchers calculate that for each additional soda consumed, the risk of obesity increases 1.6 times.

70% of Cardiovascular disease is related to obesity

42% of breast and colon cancer is diagnosed in obese individuals

30% of gall bladder surgery is related to obesity

DISSOLVES TOOTH ENAMEL

Sugar and acid in soft drinks easily dissolve tooth enamel.

When tooth decay reaches the nerve, the root, and the area at the base of the tooth, the tooth may die and, if left untreated, an abscess can develop.

HEART DISEASE

Most soft drinks contain high fructose corn syrup, a sweetener that's recently come under considerable scrutiny. High fructose corn syrup has been associated with an increased risk of metabolic syndrome, a condition associated with an elevated risk of both diabetes and heart disease.

In 2006, more than one in every four deaths were caused by heart disease.

REPRODUCTIVE ISSUES

Soft drink cans are coated with a resin that contains BPA (bisphenyl-A). This is the same cancer causing chemical found in plastic baby bottles, water bottles, and plastic containers that wreaks havoc on the endocrine system, potentially causing premature puberty and reproductive abnormalities.

99.9% of plastic bottles contain BPA.

OSTEOPOROSIS

Soft drinks contain phosphoric acid and a high phosphate diet has been associated with bone breakdown and an increased risk of osteoporosis. When phosphorus is excreted in the urine, it takes calcium with it, depriving the bones and the rest of the body of this important mineral.

Eighty percent of those affected by osteoporosis are women. Twenty percent are men.

INCREASED RISK OF DIABETES

Those who drink more soda have an 80% increased risk of developing Type 2 diabetes.

Approximately 1 in 10 health care dollars is spent on diabetes

Whole grains are made into foods like whole-wheat bread. Brown rice is another example of a whole grain. Look on food packages for a stamp that says "whole grain." You'll know you're eating healthier when you see the stamp.

Eat a Variety of Foods

People tend to divide foods into food groups. In the United States, the food groups are fruits, vegetables, grains, dairy, and protein (meat, beans, nuts, tofu).

Every food group has different nutrients in it. You should eat food from each group every day to get all the different nutrients you need. One meal should have at least three different food groups in it.

If you only ate one food for the rest of your life, you wouldn't be very healthy. Even if that food was healthy—like an orange—you wouldn't be getting the nutrients the food doesn't have. An orange has vitamin C, fiber, and some sugar, and that's good. But an orange *doesn't have* protein, vitamin B, or healthy fats.

Besides, eating oranges every day would be boring. Varying your food makes eating more fun!

Skip the Soda

How often do you drink soda? Once a week? Every day? Three times a day? If you drink soda too often, you're not doing yourself any favors.

Soda doesn't have many nutrients in it. What it does have is calories and sugar. One 20 ounce bottle of Coke® has 240 calories in it and 65 grams of sugar. Soda has empty calories—calories that don't come along with good nutrients like vitamins and minerals. In addition, that one can of Coke has two to three times more sugar than people are supposed to eat in just one day!

Cutting out soda will cut out extra calories and sugar. Save soda for special occasions. Instead, drink water, 100 percent fruit juice, or milk. If you're craving something fizzy, try seltzer and mix it with some juice.

1 Serving Looks Like . . .

GRAIN PRODUCTS

1 cup of cereal flakes = fist

1 pancake = compact disc

½ cup of cooked rice, pasta, or potato = ½ baseball

1 slice of bread = cassette tape

1 piece of cornbread = bar of soap

1 Serving Looks Like . . .

VEGETABLES AND FRUIT

 1 cup of salad greens = baseball

 1 baked potato = fist

1 med. fruit = baseball

½ cup of fresh fruit = ½ baseball

¼ cup of raisins = large egg

1 Serving Looks Like . . .

DAIRY AND CHEESE

 1½ oz. cheese = 4 stacked dice or 2 cheese slices

½ cup of ice cream = ½ baseball

FATS

1 tsp. margarine or spreads = 1 dice

1 Serving Looks Like . . .

MEAT AND ALTERNATIVES

3 oz. meat, fish, and poultry = deck of cards

3 oz. grilled/baked fish = checkbook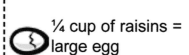

 2 Tbsp. peanut butter = ping pong ball

This chart can help you remember some serving sizes and keep your portions under control. Watching your portion sizes is a great way to make sure you're not eating too much.

Keeping Portions Small

Portions are how much of a food we choose to eat at one time. For most of us, portions tend to be big. In other words, we eat more than we really need to.

Big portions equal too many calories. One out of three kids and two out of three adults weigh too much. Part of the reason for this is that many people in America eat too much food, including fast food.

While eating, pay attention to when you're full. Stop eating before you feel stuffed. Your body takes a few minutes to realize it's full. In those few minutes, you could stuff more food into your stomach than you need.

No matter where you are, keep portions small. When you're eating dinner at home, only take a small portion at first. If you're still hungry, you can take more. Don't let yourself eat a whole bag of chips or five cookies at once.

Each meal you eat should be between 500 and 600 calories. They'll fill you up without going overboard and leave room for a couple of snacks during the day. Snacks also shouldn't be more than a couple hundred calories.

Have an Open Mind

Eating healthy is not yucky! It keeps your body working right and makes you feel good. Healthy foods are also delicious, once you try them.

So keep an open mind about healthy eating. Try new foods you've never eaten before. Retry ones you thought you didn't like.

Think about all the foods you don't like. Have you ever really given them a chance? You might think you don't like cauliflower, but when is the last time you tried it? If the answer is never, try it now! If you tried it years ago, try it again, this time with an open mind.

Scientists say people have to try new foods several times before they like them. So even if you don't like that cauliflower, give it a few more chances. You'll probably learn to like it, and will have another healthy food choice to pick from.

Enjoying food and being healthy can go hand in hand. Making cooking and healthy eating fun is an important part of staying healthy over time.

HEALTHY FAST FOODS

Ask your parents for permission to experiment with cooking your own healthy foods. Stir-fry, grill, or bake your own vegetables and meat. Try new spices that make your food flavorful. Check out recipes online or in cookbooks. You'll find it's easy to eat healthy once you know it's tasty. And even at fast-food places, you can choose to eat healthier.

4

Making Healthy Fast-Food Choices

Y ou don't have to give up fast food entirely. Now that you know the health consequences of eating fast food, you can make better decisions about it. You might decide to start ordering healthier items from the menu. Or limiting how often you visit fast-food places. Both are steps to a healthier you!

GOOD	BAD
BROILED	FRIED
STEAMED	BATTERED
BLACKENED	BUTTERY
BAKED	CREAMY
ROASTED	CRISPY
LIGHT	CHEESY
FRESH	THICK
GRILLED	BREADED
SAUTEED	SMOTHERED

Sometimes the words on the menu can tell you whether a food is healthy or not. Watch for words that might mean extra salt, sugar, or fat.

Ordering Healthy

At a fast-food restaurant, some menu choices are healthier than others. Learn how to tell what the best choices are.

Keep these guidelines in mind: eat more fruits and vegetables. Limit calories, salt, sugar, and fat. Choose smaller portions.

What do those guidelines look like at a fast-food restaurant? Well, fast-food restaurants aren't known for their fruits and vegetables, but more and more fast-food places are adding healthier choices to their menus. Whenever you can, order them. Add extra veggies on your hamburger or taco. Order a salad with lettuce, spinach, tomatoes, and other veggies. Get the fruit-and-nut parfait. (Remember, raspberry-flavored ice cream doesn't count!)

Best Choices

Next time you're at a fast-food restaurant, choose these options for the healthiest meal:

- Burger King: small hamburger, small unsalted french fries, apple fries, milk
- KFC: honey BBQ sandwich, grilled chicken breast, corn on the cob, green beans, mashed potatoes, coleslaw
- McDonald's: 4-piece chicken McNuggets® with sweet and sour sauce, small hamburger, honey mustard grilled snack wrap, small fruit and walnut salad
- Subway: 6-inch veggie delight sub, apple slices, baked chips
- Taco Bell: Fresco Style grilled steak soft taco, Fresco Style Tostada, Fresco Bean Burrito
- Wendy's: chili, garden salad with vinaigrette dressing

Soda is a big source of extra calories. You might not even notice that you're drinking hundreds of calories when you have soda with your fast food. Choosing water or milk is a healthier food choice.

Avoid fried foods. Lots of the choices at fast-food places are fried—french fries, fried chicken, onion rings, fried fish. Although fried foods are tasty, they are full of fat and extra calories. Stick with choices that are grilled or baked. For example, choose grilled chicken on that salad instead of fried chicken.

For salad dressings, choose vinaigrettes and Italian dressing. For dips, choose BBQ sauce, ketchup, and mustard. Skip ranch, blue cheese, and other creamy dressings that have extra fat and calories in them.

Pay attention to drinks, not just food. Skip the soda. Choose 100 percent juice or milk instead, or just get water to wash your food down.

Finally, remember to keep portion sizes small. People get in trouble when they order the extra-large size at fast-food places. A small side of french fries is way more reasonable than a jumbo order of fries. Small sizes let you get a taste without going overboard, while large sizes add in many extra calories. A small order of fries might only have 150 calories, but a large might have 500. And the large size also has a lot more fat and salt in it than the small size.

Order off the snack menu at places like McDonald's. If you're set on going to get fast food, ordering smaller sizes is the best way to make healthier choices.

Make Your Own!

Fast food is fast. People order fast food because they don't have a lot of time. Your mom or dad is working late, or you have to go to soccer practice or dance class. So even though the healthiest option would be to sit down at your kitchen table and eat a home-cooked meal, sometimes that just isn't possible. So what should you do?

One option is for you and your family to think ahead. You can still enjoy a fast meal without going to a fast-food restaurant if you cook meals on the weekends and freeze or refrigerate them ahead of time. You can even pack each meal up in an individual container for one person. All you have to do is take a meal and heat it up. When you only have fifteen minutes to eat, you still get a home-cooked meal.

Freeze some homemade macaroni and cheese, or some soup. Make a huge stir-fry on the weekend, and put it in the fridge for the next few days. When you're ready to eat, take

Keeping food in the fridge is a great way to make a few meals ahead of time. That way, you won't have to spend much time preparing your next meal, making the choice to eat at home much easier.

out a container and warm up the food in the microwave. Eating like this is just as fast as fast food, and you don't even have to take time to stop at a restaurant.

Meals made fresh at home don't have to take forever either. Plenty of meals only take a few minutes to make, and they don't have to be frozen dinners or boxed meals. Pasta doesn't take very long, for example. Cook whole-wheat pasta, and then add pesto or tomato sauce (from a can, or homemade and frozen). Add some cut up cooked veggies like spinach or mushrooms. Preparation will only take half an hour or less. Salads and stir-fried vegetables don't take long either. Just toss ingredients together and eat! Cooking can be easy and fast.

If you know you'll be away from home during a mealtime, pack a meal to take with you. For example, bring some dinner to eat on the way to practice. You can pack the same sorts of things that go in school lunches, like soups, sandwiches, and salads.

You can actually make your own, healthier versions of fast food at home. Look up recipes online or in cookbooks. Then you can enjoy the flavor of fast food, but not get all the extra unhealthy stuff in there.

Do Some Research

Fast-food restaurants all have websites. And most of those websites have nutrition information about all the foods served in that restaurant.

Find out how many calories your favorite hamburger has, along with how many grams of fat, salt, and sugar. Some of the things you find out might surprise you! You'll also find ingredient lists. If you've ever wondered what exactly is in those chicken nuggets, now's your chance to find out.

Sometimes the restaurant itself even has nutrition information. Look for brochures along the walls. Panera Bread even has calorie information right on the menu on the wall. Ask the cashier if you don't see any nutrition facts.

Websites and brochures should list all the same things a nutrition label on a food package does. Nutrition labels on foods at the grocery store tell you everything that's in a food, from calories, to nutrients, to ingredients. You won't find the same information on the wrapper of each cheeseburger you eat, but you can go to a website and find out the same information.

Making your favorite fast foods at home is a great way to know what you're eating and is a much healthier food choice than going to the drive-through!

Use your new knowledge to make good decisions. Is it a good idea to eat a burger with half the sodium you need in a day? Or large fries with 500 calories? More knowledge about fast foods' health effects will help you make better decisions.

Challenge yourself to eat less fast food and eat more healthy foods—and watch what happens. Pretty soon you'll be looking and feeling better than ever before!

Two Homemade Fast Foods

Try out these recipes to replace your favorite fast foods.

Burritos

Use whole wheat or corn tortillas. Cook meat or beans with spices, like chili powder, cumin, oregano, or cayenne pepper. Put veggies on top, like lettuce, diced tomatoes, cooked peppers and onions, mushrooms, or anything else you want. Add a little bit of cheese, salsa, or guacamole and roll the whole thing up. Eat it right away, or wrap it in plastic wrap and freeze for later.

Chicken Nuggets

Cut up chicken breasts into small pieces. Put breadcrumbs (preferably whole wheat) or unsweetened corn flakes into a sandwich bag, along with a little flour and salt and pepper. Beat an egg in a bowl, and dip each chicken piece in the egg. Then add the chicken to the sandwich bag, seal the bag, and shake. Make sure each piece of chicken gets covered with breadcrumbs. Take the chicken pieces out of the bag and put them on a pan to bake in the oven at 375 degrees for about fifteen minutes.

Find Out More

Online

Fast Food Nutrition Facts
www.fastfoodnutrition.org

KidsHealth: Eating Well While Eating Out
www.kidshealth.org/teen/food_fitness/nutrition/eating_out.html#cat119

LetsMove!
www.letsmove.gov/eat-healthy

In Books

Libal, Autumn. *Fats, Sugars, and Empty Calories: The Fast Food Habit.* Broomall, Penn.: Mason Crest Publishing, 2004.

Schlosser, Eric. *Chew on This: Everything You Didn't Want to Know About Fast Food.* New York: Houghton Mifflin, 2006.

Stern, Sam. *Real Food, Real Fast.* Somerville, Mass.: Candlewick Press, 2008.

Index

About the Author & Consultant

Kim Etingoff lives in Boston, Massachusetts, spending part of her time working on farms. Kim has written a number of books for young people on topics including health, history, nutrition, and business.

Dr. Borus graduated from the Harvard Medical School and the Harvard School of Public Health. He completed a residency in Pediatrics and then served as Chief Resident at Floating Hospital for Children at Tufts Medical Center before completing a fellowship in Adolescent Medicine at Boston Children's Hospital. He is currently an attending physician in the Division of Adolescent and Young Adult Medicine at Boston Children's Hospital and an Instructor of Pediatrics at Harvard Medical School.

Picture Credits